WORLD FAITHS

JUDAISM

All year dates are given using the
Christian conventions B.C. (Before
Christ) and A.D. (Anno Domini), simply
for universality of understanding

The publishers would like to thank the
following editorial consultants for their help:
Dr. Nicholas de Lange, Fellow, Wolfson College,
Cambridge, England
Rabbi Sylvia Rothschild, Bromley and
District Reform Synagogue, England
Alan Plancey

KINGFISHER
a Houghton Mifflin Company imprint
222 Berkeley Street
Boston, Massachusetts 02116
www.houghtonmifflinbooks.com

First published as *The Kingfisher Book of Religions* in 1999
This revised and updated edition published in 2005

2 4 6 8 10 9 7 5 3 1

1TR/0405/SHENS/MA(MA)/158MA

LIBRARY OF CONGRESS CATALOGING-IN-PUBLICATION DATA
has been applied for.

ISBN 0-7534-5883-7
ISBN 978-07534-5883-9

Color separations by Modern Age
Printed in Taiwan

WORLD FAITHS

JUDAISM

Worship, festivals, and ceremonies from around the world

TREVOR BARNES

KINGFISHER

BOSTON

Contents

INTRODUCTION

J udaism is the world's oldest monotheistic religion—that is to
say, it is the first of the world's great faiths to accept as its central
belief that there is only one god who created the world and who
continues to rule over it. Judaism began with Abraham, who can
properly be called the first Jew. God promised Abraham that, in return
for his obedience, Abraham would become the patriarch (father) of a
great nation. God commanded Abraham to leave his home (Ur of the
Chaldees in present-day Iraq between the Tigris and Euphrates rivers)
and to travel to a land that God had promised him—Israel. Abraham
agreed, thus accepting the Covenant (agreement) that God had made
with him and, by extension, with the people of Israel. As a sign of the
Covenant, even today, every male Jew has to be circumcised.

Revelation on Mount Sinai

According to the Hebrew Bible, the word of God was revealed to
Moses on Mount Sinai some 3,500 years ago. It is said that at that
moment God handed over not only the Ten Commandments but also
the first five books of scripture,
known as the Torah.
The ancient Israelites
are said to have chosen
to accept the honor
and responsibility of the
Covenant at the same
time that God is said to
have chosen them. Hence,
they and their descendants
consider themselves to be
"The Chosen People."

From tribe to nation

The "Israelites" began
as a small family, forced
into slavery in Egypt,
then wandering in the
desert before arriving
in the Promised Land of
Canaan, where King Saul,
and then King David,
built them into a nation.

Above This boy is carrying the Torah
scrolls to a service, where they will focus
the hearts and minds of the congregation
on the word of God. On their thirteenth
birthdays, boys are allowed to read from
the Torah scrolls for the first time.

Left This Jewish Ethiopian boy is
holding the scrolls. The Jews are not
a race. They are best described as a
people or a family from many different
races and lands united by a shared
sense of belief and tradition.

Around 950 B.C., David's son, Solomon, built a magnificent Temple. It was destroyed in 586 B.C. by the Babylonians, who took the Jews into captivity. A second Temple was built, but this was destroyed by the Romans in A.D. 70, leading to another great dispersal (*diaspora*) of the Jews throughout the Middle East and Europe.

Unity in adversity

Despite the fact that the Jews were spread far and wide, they tried—not always successfully—to stay true to God's law. Eventually, the interpretations of the law contained in the Torah were debated and written down by the rabbis (teachers) and gathered together into a collection of writings known as the Talmud. Study of the Talmud helped to give a unity to Jewish practice.

Death and regeneration

The biggest challenge to the Jewish people in the modern age came in the late 1930s, when the Nazis, under Adolf Hitler, began what they hoped would be the complete extermination of the Jews. More than six million Jews were murdered in what has come to be called the Holocaust. And yet, although comparatively few in number (today there are only some 12 million worldwide), the Jews have exerted a spiritual, ethical, and intellectual influence out of all proportion to their numbers. Their religious practices have been adapted to suit modern times, but the core of the Jewish faith recalls a pivotal event—when the ancient Israelites were said to have submitted themselves to the word of God and were inspired to lead their lives by it.

Right *The Star of David was first used as a symbol of Jewish identity in the 1300s. It was originally used as a magical sign in the Middle East, where it was known as Solomon's Seal.*

THE HISTORY OF JUDAISM

Judaism began with Abraham, who was uncomfortable with the many pagan gods of his homeland in Mesopotamia and responded to the call of the one true God to leave home. The story of his departure is contained in the first book of scripture (Genesis 12:1), where God says, "Leave your country, your people, and your father's household, and go to the land I will show you." Abraham's grandson Jacob (later named Israel by God) had 12 sons whose families became the 12 tribes of Israel. Several generations later, the twelve tribes were taken into slavery by the Egyptians. Eventually, they were led out of Egypt—in what is known as the Exodus—by Moses, who later received God's Ten Commandments on Mount Sinai. After 40 long years of wandering in the desert, the Israelites entered the "Promised Land" of Canaan—led not by Moses, who did not live to take them there, but by his brother Joshua. The Israelites grew in strength and, after rule by leaders known as Judges, looked for a king to govern.

A nation divided

The Bible describes the Israelites hope that this king, ritually blessed and anointed, would triumph over their enemies and establish a kingdom in which divine justice. prevailed. The succession of kings anointed in this way (beginning with Saul) symbolized the Jewish expectation that God's righteousness would eventually be a reality on Earth. King David made Jerusalem his capital. His son Solomon built the first Temple there. When Solomon died (c.930 B.C.), the nation was split into two by an internal rebellion. Jeroboam and ten of the 12 tribes established the Kingdom of Israel in the north, while the descendants of Rehoboam founded Judah in the south.

Above The great rebellion against the Romans ended at Masada, a desert fortress by the Dead Sea. Rather than surrender, the entire camp committed suicide. Masada has since become a symbol of heroism and resistance.

Left The menorah (a candlestick with seven branches) was first used in the Tabernacle in the desert and later installed in Solomon's Temple, Jerusalem.

8

There was great tension between the prophets and the kings. The prophets criticized their rulers for worshiping false idols and for straying from the path of God. The Kingdom of Judah (from which Judaism takes its name) outlived that of Israel, whose ten tribes vanished from history. But Judah was itself overrun by the Babylonians, who captured the Jews and destroyed the Temple in 586 B.C.

Above *According to scripture, David killed the giant Goliath, a warrior of the Philistines, with a single slingshot. David eventually became king of the Israelites and made Jerusalem his capital city.*

Exile and return

Fifty years later, the Babylonians were themselves captured by the Persians, who gave the Jews permission to return home. Some Jews did so and they began to rebuild the Temple. Others stayed in Babylon until around 458 B.C. when, under Jewish leaders Ezra and Nehemiah, they returned and put the law of the Torah and worship of God at the center of their religious and political lives.

In the next centuries, further invasions threatened to destroy Jewish identity with Greek philosophy and with pagan forms of worship. In 165 B.C., Judas Maccabeus led a revolt against the Syrians and restored the Temple to its original purity. This victory is remembered each year in the festival of Chanukah (*see* page 103).

Below *Moses, a towering figure in Jewish history, leads his people out of slavery in Egypt. Behind the Israelites, Pharaoh's army drowns in the Red Sea.*

Dispersal

The country came under Roman control in 63 B.C. This was hard to accept and the Jews mounted a series of rebellions that ended in A.D. 135. In A.D. 70, the Romans had destroyed Jerusalem and its Temple and killed many of the inhabitants. Other Jews dispersed throughout the Middle East and Europe, and developed their own religious life, many hoping that one day they would return to their homeland. The State of Israelwas finally founded in 1948.

THE CHOSEN PEOPLE

The ancient region of Mesopotamia in the fertile crescent of land between the Tigris and Euphrates rivers was home to many civilizations and religions. The Assyrians, the Sumerians, the Akkadians, and the Babylonians had elaborate belief systems and worshipped many gods.

There were gods of the Sun, Moon, and stars, in addition to lesser gods who were believed to be responsible for different areas of life such as for crops, animals, rainfall, and fertility. Clay statues were made to honor these gods and were placed in temples and houses to bring protection and good fortune in life. It was into such a society that Abraham was born around 4,000 years ago.

An adventure into the unknown

The Hebrew Bible tells us that God spoke to Abraham and promised him that he and his descendants would eventually become a great nation. Abraham heard the call and left his homeland with its pagan gods to embark into the unknown on a journey of faith.

In one sense God "chose" Abraham above all the other tribes and nations at the time. But in another sense Abraham "chose" to follow the word of the one true God. Being "chosen" does not imply superiority, but it does involve responsibility to follow God's will.

The promise to Abraham was expressed in terms of a "covenant," a contract or agreement, which was also used at the time to describe a treaty between tribes and nations. The terms of the covenant were that in return for Abraham's obedience God would bless his people. Disobedience, however, would eventually exact a heavy price.

Above Abraham's willingness to sacrifice his son, Isaac, shows how far he was prepared to go to remain faithful to God. This painting is by the Dutch artist Rembrandt (1606–1669).

Right Abraham's journey from his homeland in Ur is described in the Book of Genesis. However, there are a number of conflicting accounts of the precise route that he took.

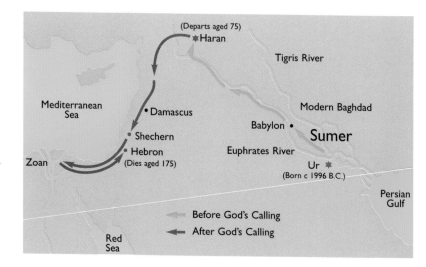

(Departs aged 75)
Haran

Tigris River

Mediterranean Sea

Damascus

Modern Baghdad

Babylon

Sumer

Shechern

Euphrates River

Hebron
(Dies aged 175)

Zoan

Ur
(Born c 1996 B.C.)

Persian Gulf

Red Sea

→ Before God's Calling
← After God's Calling

Above The desert landscape of Israel has changed little over 3,500 years. On their long journey to the Promised Land Abraham and his family would have set up shelter much like this bedouin encampment.

Wandering

The journey to the Promised Land of Canaan was neither easy nor direct. At one stage due to lack of food, the Israelites were forced to settle in Egypt. At first they were respected as useful immigrants who could play an important role in the life of the ountry. But after many generations they were viewed as unwelcome and threatening outsiders and were made to work as the Egyptians' slaves.

Through God's power and under the guidance of their towering leader, Moses, they eventually achieved their freedom but were forced to wander through the desert for 40 years before arriving in the Promised Land. After the death of Moses the Israelites entered the land of Canaan under the leadership of Joshua.

Above Jerusalem was captured by King David in the 900s B.C. and became both the political and spiritual capital of ancient Israel.

The Promised Land

By 1,000 B.C., as promised, the people of Israel had become a great nation and had built the magnificent Temple in Jerusalem to honor God for his blessings. However, in 586 B.C. "King David's City" was captured by the Babylonians, and the Temple was destroyed. Many Israelites were taken into captivity believing that this was a punishment for drifting away from God's laws. However, 50 years later they returned to Jerusalem and rebuilt the Temple, which was to stand for more than 500 years until its destruction again by the Romans in A.D. 70.

TWO KINGDOMS

Israel's first king, Saul, was a great warrior, but a flawed ruler. His successor, King David, united the different tribes and established Jerusalem as the new nation's capital. His son, Solomon, built on these achievements and constucted the magnificent Temple to house the Ark of the Covenant containing the stone tablets engraved with the Ten Commandments.

Jerusalem became not only the nation's political capital, but also its spiritual heart. The Temple was a monument to the one true God and a reminder to the people and to the world that obedience to the Almighty was central to the very survival of Israel.

Rebellion

After the death of Solomon his son, Rehoboam, ascended the throne but was soon facing a challenge to his authority from a man in the north named Jeroboam. Jeroboam gathered ten of the original 12 tribes around him and split from the southern Kingdom of Judah to found a new Kingdom of Israel. The nation was now divided.

Envious of the splendor of Jerusalem and its elaborate Temple, Jeroboam began to set up rival shrines dedicated to the worship of idols in the form of golden calves. This was exactly what God had warned against. The later reign of King Ahab and his wife Jezebel also marked a low point in Israel's spiritual life. Corruption and godlessness were everywhere and were a cause of great concern for the prophet Elijah (and his successor Elisha), who repeatedly thundered out warnings of God's growing anger.

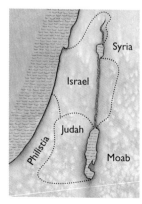

Left *Jeroboam's rebellion divided the kingdom in two, with Israel in the north and Judah in the south. Judah survived and was renamed Israel.*

Right *This statue of the god Baal dates from between 1400 and 1200 B.C. It would have been worshipped by many of the peoples of the Near East at the time of Abraham.*

"For so it was that the children of Israel had sinned against the Lord, their God."

II Kings 17:7

A kingdom destroyed

Invasion by the Assyrians under King Sargon II saw the end of the Kingdom of Israel. Tens of thousands of people were rounded up and taken into captivity. The rulers and their people had paid a heavy price for their wicked behavior and disobedience. The Ten Tribes of Israel simply disappeared and vanished from history.

Judah

The southern Kingdom of Judah survived longer and eventually took the name of the northern kingdom, Israel. But it, too, was threatened by foreign invaders—the Babylonians—who destroyed the Temple in 586 B.C. and took many of the people into captivity.

The people of Israel took this as another sign of God's displeasure, remembering that they had been told that their obedience to his laws would be rewarded and their disobedience punished. But even in exile they were encouraged by prophets, such as Ezekiel, to return to the word of God and to prepare themselves for a return to their land when the Temple would be rebuilt.

Left The southern Kingdom of Judah eventually fell to the Babylonians who took its people into captivity. This painting by Herbert Schmaltz shows their sadness in exile from their homeland.

PATRIARCHS, PROPHETS, AND KINGS

Throughout the 4,000 years of its history, Judaism has produced a number of powerful individuals who have made their mark on the faith and shaped it into what it is today.

Abraham, Isaac, and Jacob

The first of the patriarchs was Abraham, whose story is told in the Book of Genesis (which is partly an early tribal history of the people of Israel). Around 2000 B.C., Abraham left the city of Ur of the Chaldees to go where God chose to send him. Abraham was 75 years old, and although he and his wife Sarah had no children he was told that he would father a great nation. When Abraham was 100 years old, he and Sarah had their first child, Isaac, who was very precious to Abraham because he would be the next in line to carry out God's plan. According to the Hebrew Bible, Abraham was commanded to sacrifice Isaac as proof of his obedience to God. With a heavy heart Abraham agreed, but at the last moment God intervened and, praising Abraham for his faithfulness, spared Isaac and ordered Abraham to sacrifice a ram instead.

Isaac had twin sons—Jacob and Esau. Jacob had a dream one night in which he saw angels climbing a ladder into heaven and heard God promising him and his family the land on which they slept. Many years later Jacob met a stranger who challenged Jacob to wrestle with him through the night. The stranger revealed himself as another angel of God, and told Jacob that from now on he would be called Israel, which means "one who strives with God." The 12 tribes that formed the nation of Israel (*see* page 88) are said to have descended from Jacob's (Israel's) 12 sons.

Above *As a sign of obedience, God commanded Abraham to sacrifice his son Isaac. At the last moment, when he was sure of Abraham's faithfulness, God intervened and spared Isaac.*

Left *Isaiah and the other prophets of the Hebrew Bible criticized immoral and ungodly behavior. They constantly challenged people—even those in power—to walk the path of righteousness.*

Above Jacob, who was later renamed Israel, had a dream of angels ascending a ladder to heaven. This painting is from the Christian Lambeth Bible (c.1140–50).

"Behold, I have set the land before you: go in and possess the land which the Lord swore unto your fathers, Abraham, Isaac, and Jacob."

Deuteronomy 1:8

Moses and David

Moses is the next major figure to shape the ancient Israelite experience. According to the Torah, Moses led the Israelites out of slavery in Egypt, and following a unique experience with God, he handed on to the people enduring laws govering worship and daily life. Once in the Promised Land, the Israelites submitted themselves to the authority of anointed kings, whom they hoped would rule justly. Their first great king was David, a warrior and musician credited with writing some of the Psalms—the sacred hymns of the Hebrew Bible.

The prophets

Over the years, the kings and the people ignored God's teachings and were criticized for their bad behavior by the prophets. Isaiah was a prophet of Judah in the 700s B.C., at a time when many felt that some of the rich people were lazy in their worship and unjust to the poor. Isaiah told them that God would punish Judah if they did not improve their ways. Jeremiah was a pessimistic prophet who foretold the destruction of Jerusalem. Other minor prophets spoke on similar themes: that faithfulness to God and a life of holiness are the most important things, and the consequences of sin and disobedience can be severe.

15

THE TEMPLE

After King David turned Jerusalem into a great city, his son Solomon built the first Temple and established Jerusalem as the geographical and spiritual capital of his kingdom.

The Ark of the Covenant

At the core of the Temple was the Holy of Holies, the sanctuary where the Ark of the Covenant, a chest containing the Ten Commandments, was placed. The chest was carried by the ancient Israelites as they wandered through the desert toward the Promised Land, and it was their most precious possession. The Temple gave it a permanent home. So sacred were the Ark and its contents that only the High Priest could enter the sanctuary, and only once a year, on the Day of Atonement, Yom Kippur.

Building the Temple

The construction of the Temple is described in detail in the Book of Kings. The wood is said to have come from the cedar trees of Lebanon, or from fir and olive groves, and it was carved with tiny flowers to form the floor, walls, and roof beams. The stone structure was, in fact, carved elsewhere and assembled on site so that the sound of hammers and chisels would not disturb the sacred place. Construction of the Temple ("house" in the Hebrew Bible) was proof that the Jews were serving God who, in return, would bless them. Precious stones and metals were used in the construction, and even the hinges of the door leading to the Holy of Holies were made from gold.

At the back of the Temple there were steps that led to the Holy of Holies, where the Ark of the Covenant was kept.

Before they were sacrificed, lambs were washed in wheeled basins of water.

Left This view of Jerusalem shows the Dome of the Rock and the Western (Wailing) Wall in the foreground.

16

Below *The Temple, built by King Solomon, was the spiritual center of Jerusalem and of the kingdom. It was not just one building, but a series of buildings ringed by courtyards. The outer courtyard was open to everyone, including non-Jews (Gentiles), but the rest of the space was reserved for Jews only. The inner courtyard of the priests is shown here.*

Sacrificial lambs were slaughtered at the altar. To this day, a lamb shankbone is eaten on Passover in commemoration of this ritual sacrifice.

Temple worship

Temple worship was extremely ritualistic and involved sacrifice and elaborate rites performed by priests. Later, some of the priests were criticized by the prophets for putting the form of the ritual above the content of God's message. The prophets felt that no amount of sacrifice or incense would compensate for ungodly behavior; if people sinned against God or other people by lying, stealing, or killing, they felt God would punish them.

Above *The largest remaining section of the Temple Mount is the Western Wall. Jews come here to say their prayers, facing the Wall and bowing ritually.*

Destruction of the Temple

The Temple was destroyed in 586 B.C., rebuilt after the Babylonian exile, and extended under King Herod the Great, before its final destruction in A.D. 70. Today, the remaining Western Wall is the most sacred site in the Jewish world. Jews recite their prayers at the Wall or write them down on slips of paper that they insert into the cracks between the stones. The Western Wall is sometimes called the Wailing Wall because of the cries of devout Jews lamenting the destruction of the Temple. Traditionally, it is said that when the Messiah comes the Temple will be built again and that God's Kingdom of righteousness will come to Earth. When the Temple was finally destroyed, temple worship came to an end and local synagogues took its place.

THE TORAH

The Torah is the name given to the first five books of the Hebrew Bible—Genesis, Exodus, Leviticus, Numbers, and Deuteronomy. They are believed by traditional Jews to be the word of God as revealed to Moses on Mount Sinai. Progressive or liberal Jews believe that the word of God was not revealed at one particular time, but is part of a continuing process that successive generations work out under God's inspiration.

The Ten Commandments

As well as creation stories, Jewish history, poetry, and family sagas, the first five books also contain the Ten Commandments. These set out the basic principles that even non-Jewish societies should follow for their own good. In addition to this, they set down religious and moral codes that Jews should follow if they wish to do God's will.

Personal morality

The Ten Commandments are central to the Torah, but many other important rules are found within the five books. These are the basis of 613 *mitzvot* (commandments), which cover areas of personal morality, such as loving your neighbor as yourself, or treating people with respect. The *mitzvot* govern relationships between husband and wife, and between parents and children. They state what rituals Jews should carry out, what they should wear, how they should worship, how animals should be slaughtered, and what foods can and cannot be eaten.

***Above** The five Books of Moses are copied by hand onto parchment and made into scrolls brought out for weekly synagogue worship.*

***Right** Studying the Torah is the work of a lifetime.*

Left *The study of the Torah is central to Jewish faith. Students are encouraged to read and re-read it in order to understand how God's law can be put into practice in everyday life.*

The "Oral Torah"

As well as the five books known as the "Written Torah," Moses is also thought by traditional Jews to have received from God the "Oral Torah." This is the ongoing interpretation of the laws contained in the written Torah—laws debated and questioned by rabbis down the generations. It instructs Jews on how they are to live a life pleasing to God, as an example to the world.

> ## "I am the Lord your God ... You shall have no other gods before me."
>
> God to Moses on Mount Sinai, Exodus 20.2–3

A place of honor

As a reminder of how sacred it is to the Jewish people, a copy of the Torah, handwritten on special scrolls, is kept in a container called an ark in every synagogue. Rabbis argue over the exact meaning of the text. Traditional Jews believe that the Torah, being divinely inspired, is as valid today as it was in the ancient world. Those who take a more liberal view say that some of the strict rules have to be adapted for Jews to come to terms with the modern world.

Left *Moses is traditionally said to have received the Ten Commandments directly from God on Mount Sinai. These established a framework of law on which a civilized society could be built.*

THE TEN COMMANDMENTS
Exodus Chapter 20, verses 2–17

1. I am the Lord your God. You shall have no other gods before me.
2. You shall not make a graven image.
3. You shall not take the name of the Lord your God in vain.
4. Keep the Sabbath Day holy. Do not work on the Sabbath.
5. Honor your father and mother.
6. You shall not kill.
7. You shall not commit adultery.
8. You shall not steal.
9. You shall not bear false witness.
10. You shall not covet your neighbor's property.

JEWISH WORSHIP

With the destruction of the Temple in A.D. 70, worship gradually centred on the synagogue, which originally meant "meeting-place." Worship, or *avodah* in Hebrew, implies service to the Creator and was referred to by the ancient rabbis as "the service of the heart," that is to say, something done willingly and joyfully to give thanks for the divine gift of life.

Synagogue worship

Devout Jews attend the synagogue three times a day, in the morning, afternoon, and evening—in a pattern that recalls the now vanished ritual of the Temple. In the morning and evening they recite the *Shema*. This is a group of three readings from the Torah, beginning with the words, "Hear O Israel, the Lord is our God, the Lord is One." The *Shema* is the basic affirmation of the Jewish faith.

For a full Orthodox service to take place, ten men need to be present—a minimum requirement for communal worship, known as a *minyan*. At the heart of the service is a series of blessings called the *Amidah*, which the congregation recites while standing. While Orthodox men and women sit separated by a balcony or other divider, non-Orthodox men, women, and children generally worship together.

Above A child lights the candles of a menorah, a branched candlestick, used to celebrate Chanukah.

The day of rest

The focal-point of the Jewish week is the Sabbath (*Shabbat*), the day of rest that the Ten Commandments decree should be kept holy. The Sabbath begins on Friday evening at sunset, and families frequently make a last-minute dash to prepare and cook the meal that ushers it in. Many Sabbath observances center on the home.

Right The Shabbat meal has preserved Jewish identity. Here the blessing of wine and bread is made at the Sabbath table.

An act of worship

The beginning of the Sabbath is traditionally marked by the lighting of candles, followed by a special meal. A blessing is made over the wine and bread, and the family sits down together to eat in commemoration of the creation of the world and the deliverance of the people of Israel out of slavery in Egypt. The family meal is an act of worship in itself—when the food is blessed, the table becomes an altar, emphasizing its importance as a spiritual focus. This domestic event has kept the Jewish identity intact in the most hostile circumstances.

The Torah gives practical instructions for observing the Sabbath, and the "Oral Torah" is even more explicit. No work is permitted, and the definition of work extends to activities such as driving and sewing—although an exception is made to all these rules if someone's life is in danger. For some Jews, simply switching on a light is considered work. However, many Jews do not consider these restrictions to be an inconvenience. Instead, they have devices such as time switches that allow electric appliances to come on automatically during the Sabbath, which liberate them from the working week and allow everyone in the family to spend more time in worship, study, or conversation.

Above *According to Jewish law, Jews must ritually wash their hands at certain times, such as before eating.*

Below *When praying in the synagogue, male Jews wear a* yarmulke, *or skullcap, as a sign of respect to God.*

STUDYING THE LAW

The Hebrew Bible is not a book like any other. Many Jews believe it contains the basis for all there is to know in order to live a godly life. In particular, they base their lives on the revealed word of God, said to have been handed down in the form of the Torah on Mount Sinai. The Torah, as we have seen, comprises the first five books of the Hebrew Bible and contains 613 commandments, or *mitzvot*, which pious Jews seek to study, to understand, and to follow.

The tradition of scholarship
Study of these texts, which has exercised the minds of the most brilliant scholars in Jewish history, is the work of a lifetime, but every Jew is expected to spend some time studying the Torah. From an early age children are taught what the commandments are and are shown, through study and example, how to carry them out. At first they learn from their parents in the home, then from their teachers at the synagogue. Boys may also go to a *yeshiva*, or religious academy, where they will study the scriptures into their early twenties. Although study and debate are intense, the atmosphere is relaxed and informal. Orthodox women are generally not expected to study the Torah. Their religious duty is primarily to care for the home and raise children. In the non-Orthodox world, women do study the Torah, and have the same expectations as men. Some become rabbis themselves—although women rabbis are not recognized by the Orthodox community.

Above *Elaborately decorated cases are used to house the Torah scrolls. The decoration does not include any human figures—in obedience of the commandment not to make a graven image.*

Oral tradition
Throughout Jewish history the Torah has been discussed endlessly, and from the earliest times interpretations have been handed down by word of mouth to the next generation. Around the A.D. 100s, Rabbi Judah ("the Prince") brought the oral traditions together in a written collection known as the *Mishnah*.

Left *This female rabbi is using a yad, or pointer, to read from the Torah. The text of the scrolls is never touched directly. The yad is used both to protect the Torah, and as a sign of its sanctity.*

> "Behold, I set before you this day a blessing and a curse. A blessing if you obey the commandments of the Lord your God and a curse if you will not obey the commandments."
>
> Deuteronomy 12:27–28
> Exodus 20:2–3

In parallel with this, another volume of commentary was being prepared. The *Midrash* is a collection of sermons, stories, and parables (*Aggadah*) told by rabbis to explain the Torah. Between A.D. 200 and 500, the *Mishnah* received its own commentary (known as the *Gemara*, or completion). Together these formed one huge collection—the Talmud, a comprehensive commentary on Jewish religious law (*Halakah*) that forms the backbone of a Jew's scholarly and religious life. It is said that in the hereafter Jews are rewarded with an eternity in the presence of Moses, discussing the finer points of the Torah.

Reverence for the Torah

While the Talmud and other commentaries are regarded as books like any others, the Torah scrolls are given a special religious status. When a service is over, the scrolls are carefully rolled up and replaced in a case, which is often richly decorated. Conditions of life have changed since the time of Moses, who could not have imagined a world of high technology, transplant surgery, genetic engineering, or space flight. But many Jews still believe that the basic laws of 3,000 years ago can be reinterpreted to apply to every circumstance today.

Left Scholarship is very important in the Jewish tradition. Study of the Talmud begins at an early age.

The Jewish Calendar

The Jewish New Year begins with Rosh Hashanah, a time to look back on mistakes made during the previous year and to resolve to do better in the year ahead. A ram's horn (a *shofar*) is blown, and this produces a raw, piercing sound that is meant to call sinners to repentance. The Rosh Hashanah festival also commemorates God's creation and it is a time to consider how the deeds of the past year will be judged. Traditionally, Jews eat apples dipped in honey and they wish each other a sweet New Year. The next ten days are then set aside for serious reflection and preparation for Yom Kippur—the most sacred Jewish holy day.

The Day of Atonement

Yom Kippur is the culmination of the ten days of self-examination that began at Rosh Hashanah. In ancient times, this was the one day in the year when the high priest made a sacrifice to atone for the sins of the people and entered the Holy of Holies in the Jerusalem Temple, where the Ten Commandments had been placed. Today, sacrifice is no longer carried out and, instead, the Day of Atonement is focused on the synagogue, where a day-long service is held, accompanied by a 25-hour fast. When the congregation has admitted its sins, prayers are said for forgiveness. Yom Kippur is regarded as an annual opportunity for spiritual renewal.

Above For the festival of Sukkot, these Jewish school children are building temporary shelters (tabernacles or booths) as a reminder of the years that the Israelites spent wandering in the desert with only tents for shelter.

Left A family lights the Chanukah candles recalling the re-dedication of the Temple in 165 B.C. after it had been desecrated by the Syrians.

The Feast of Tabernacles

Five days after Yom Kippur, the Feast of Tabernacles, or Sukkot, takes place, when Jews remember how God provided for the Children of Israel as they wandered in the desert for 40 years before arriving in the Promised Land. As a reminder of their time in the wilderness, when they had only tents to sleep in, Jews construct temporary shelters (tabernacles or booths) at home or in the synagogue. They may eat, study, and even sleep in them. At the end of Sukkot there is a synagogue service known as Simchat Torah, or Rejoicing in the Law. The scrolls are paraded around the synagogue, to the accompaniment of joyful singing and dancing.

> "Love the Lord your God and keep . . . his laws and his commandments always."
>
> Deuteronomy 11:1

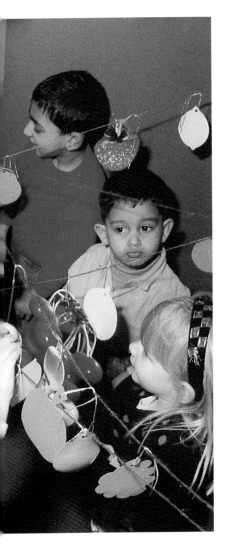

Right A shofar, or ram's horn, is blown at Rosh Hashanah to call Jews to repentance.

Remembering the past

Chanukah is a winter festival, but it celebrates more than just a seasonal cycle. It reminds Jews of the period in their history (165 B.C.) when they fought the Greek influences that threatened their identity and the purity of their Temple. Judas Maccabaeus, a member of the Hasmonean family, led a revolt against those who had desecrated the Temple. According to legend there was enough oil in the Temple lamp to last for one day, but miraculously it burned for eight days, at the end of which Judas Maccabaeus re-dedicated the Temple. In public and private ceremonies Jews celebrate the festival by lighting candles on an eight-branched *menorah*. A ninth branch holds the "servant candle" from which the rest are lit—one on the first day, two on the second, three on the third and so on, until the candlestick is ablaze with light.

JEWISH PRACTICES

Passover, or *Pesach* in Hebrew, recalls the story of the Exodus from Egypt. It takes its name from the last of the ten plagues that persuaded the pharaoh to set the Israelites free. First, the Nile River turned to blood, then there was a plague of frogs, a plague of gnats, and a plague of flies. Next, the Egyptians' cattle died, and the people were afflicted with boils. After hailstones and a plague of locusts, followed by a three-day period of darkness, the most devastating of the plagues descended. The Angel of Death "passed over" the children of Israel, but the first-born son of every Egyptian died. The pharaoh agreed to release the Israelites, who left in such a hurry that they were unable to let the bread they had prepared for their journey rise. As a result only unleavened bread (bread without yeast) can be eaten during the week of Passover. A ritual meal is prepared of foods that symbolize the flight from Egypt. Traditionally, the youngest child present asks, "Why is this night different from all other nights?", and the father tells the story of the Exodus.

Shavuot (originally a harvest festival) is celebrated 50 days after the second day of Passover and it recalls the handing over of the Torah to Moses on Mount Sinai. The Ten Commandments are read out in the synagogue, which is often decorated with flowers and fruit to celebrate the first fruits of the season.

Above Passover is as important today as it was in the time of Moses. The symbolism of the meal, here depicted in a 15th-century manuscript, has remained unchanged.

The Festival of Lots

Purim—the Festival of Lots—is a minor festival that precedes Passover. It marks the victory of Esther and her uncle Mordechai over Haman, a minister of the Persian Emperor who threatened to exterminate the Jewish people and cast lots (*purim*) to decide on which day he should carry out his threat.

THE SEDER MEAL

The ritual Passover meal is known as *seder*. Bitter herbs recall slavery, an egg and a lamb shankbone commemorate ritual sacrifice, saltwater symbolizes the tears of the Israelites, and a mixture of nuts, cinnamon, and wine represents the mortar they were forced to mix for the pharaoh's building. The unleavened bread—a dry cracker known as *matzo*—is the bread of affliction.

Right A Jewish bride and groom celebrate their wedding under the huppah(canopy) which is a symbol of God's sheltering, protective power.

Below At the age of 13, a boy comes of age and becomes a Bar Mitzvah, *or Son of the Commandment. During prayer,* Orthodox Jews wear tefillin *on their head and arms. These are small boxes containing scriptural texts.*

Rites of passage

As descendants of the patriarch Abraham, Jews belong to an ancient family, and it is as a family that they mark the great life cycle events. These begin shortly after birth, when boys are circumcised as a mark of God's covenant with Abraham. Girls receive a special blessing in a synagogue or at a service at home. Jewish boys come of age when they are 13, at a special service marking the transition into adulthood, when they become a *Bar Mitzvah*, or Son of the Commandment. Girls come of age when they are 12 and become a *Bat Mitzvah*, or Daughter of the Commandment.

Weddings are very festive occasions, with the whole community joining in the celebrations. Couples marry beneath a *huppah*, or canopy, a survival of the ancient bridal bower in which newlyweds used to be secluded after the ceremony. The groom breaks a glass beneath his foot—a reminder that life is fragile.

Jewish funerals usually take place within 24 hours of death. Relatives tear a garment as a mark of mourning and the deceased's children recite the *Kaddish*, a prayer which is a mark of mourning, but also an affirmation of life.

THIS LIFE AND BEYOND

Judaism is first and foremost a religion of the here and now. Life is to be celebrated as a gift from God. Good deeds are to be done not in expectation of a reward (in this life or the next), but because goodness and obedience to His laws are what God expects. Judaism says that these laws exist not to stop people from enjoying life but, on the contrary, to enable them to live a full life; to be aware of their rights but also of their responsibilities.

Sometimes the laws contained in the Hebrew Bible seem outdated. But the scholars and rabbis who have studied the texts over hundreds of years have tried to show their relevance. Laws about not cheating in business, for example, are as clear today as they were 3,500 years ago. Judaism says that if we are to lead the good life that God intends, then our relationship toward others requires the same commitment as our relationship to God.

Beyond the everyday
Jews believe that simple, everyday rituals contain within them a hint of God's nature. A shared meal on the eve of the Sabbath with the table prepared like a domestic altar, for example, is an opportunity to appreciate God in the day-to-day rhythm of life. A Sabbath spent doing no work at all creates a space and a silence in which God's presence can be felt and nature can be appreciated. But, similar to many people of other faiths, some individuals want to achieve a more intense relationship with God. They want to explore the spiritual world that lies behind the everyday.

Students of the mystical traditions of the Kabbalah strive for a personal experience of the divine, spending years of study on ancient texts written by those who have tried to understand the intense mystery of God.

Above The rainbow is a symbol of God's promise to Noah (Genesis 9:13) and of His covenant with humanity. Orthodox Jews will say a blessing when they see a rainbow in the sky.

Left In this Jewish cemetery on the slopes of the Mount of Olives in Jerusalem, Jews have placed stones on the graves as a mark of respect for the dead.

Right Here, Orthodox Jews celebrate a joyous occasion with dancing and singing. Judaism promotes the full enjoyment of life's proper pleasures alongside its duties and responsibilities.

The afterlife

Orthodox Jews believe in the immortality of the soul and expect the resurrection of the dead in the time of the Messiah. Jews are content to concern themselves with this life and to let the next life (whatever that means) take care of itself.

Funeral rituals are designed to deal with the powerful emotions surrounding the loss of a loved one and to help ordinary people come to terms with the pain of bereavement. After a funeral there is a seven-day period of mourning known as "shiva," during which friends and family visit the home of the bereaved and traditionally sit on low chairs as a sign of humility. For 30 days the mourners may not attend any festivities or parties as a sign of respect.

For the loss of a parent the children recite the *kaddish* in the synagogue for 11 months and mourn for a period of 12 months. The *kaddish* is a prayer essentially celebrating the glory of God, enabling Jews to move from a time of intense grief to a gradual acceptance that death is a part of life and that ultimately this life must go on.

On the anniversary of the death a special candle is lit in the home or synagogue. It burns for 24 hours during which time the *kaddish*, along with the name of the dead person, is recited at the synagogue service. It is the particular duty and responsibility of the children to say prayers on behalf of the dead parents.

Left This extract from the mystical Jewish text known as the Kabbalah uses signs and symbols to explain the nature of the Almighty.

THE DIASPORA

The destruction of the Temple by the Romans in A.D. 70 was a decisive event in the history of Judaism. At a stroke, Jews lost the unifying feature of their spiritual life—Temple worship—and were also in danger of losing their identity.

The rabbinic tradition

A decision by Johanan ben Zakkai to set up a religious academy on the Judean coast in Yavneh, however, provided a solution. The academy, staffed by rabbis or teachers, soon became a focus of learning and shared tradition within the Jewish world. Although it declined in importance after the failure of the last Jewish revolt against the Romans in A.D. 135, other academies in Galilee and Babylonia took its place and a sense of continuity was maintained.

The Golden Age

When the Roman Emperor Constantine converted to Christianity in A.D. 313, making it the state religion a decade later, life became hard for the Jews. By now, many had already dispersed, settling around the Mediterranean, especially in Spain. Persecution became commonplace and they would not know real stability until the middle of the A.D. 600s when Muslim Arab invasions transformed the map of Europe. The Jews flourished under the Moors to such an extent that the 900s and 1000s were known as Spain's "Golden Age," when philosophers and religious leaders from both Islam and Judaism shared each others' ideas and lived together in harmony.

מעל הבית נבנ ביתנ שאומרים דהודוד

Above This 14th-century illumination shows a service in a synagogue in northern Spain. Jews and Muslims lived together in harmony, and the influence of Islamic or Moorish art on the synagogue is clear.

Left The destruction of the Temple in A.D. 70 is depicted on the victory arch of Titus in Rome. Roman soldiers carry off the Temple menorah.

MAIMONIDES' 13 PRINCIPLES OF FAITH

1. God exists.
2. He is one.
3. He is unique and incorporeal (i.e., not made out of flesh and blood like humans).
4. He is eternal.
5. He alone should be worshiped.
6. The prophets spoke God's revealed word.
7. Moses was the greatest of the prophets.
8. God revealed himself to Moses and gave him the Torah.
9. Neither God nor the Torah will change.
10. God knows everything.
11. People will be rewarded for good deeds and punished for bad.
12. The Messiah will come to Earth.
13. The dead will be resurrected.

Sephardi and Ashkenazi

The *diaspora* (dispersal) of the Jews outside Israel produced two distinct traditions: the Sephardi Jews of Spain and the Mediterranean who spoke in a mixture of old Spanish and Hebrew known as Ladino, and the Ashkenazi Jews who settled in central Europe and Germany and who spoke in a mixture of German and Hebrew dialect known as Yiddish.

Philosophy and mysticism

Spain's Golden Age provided a period of stability that produced many outstanding Jewish scholars. One of these was Moses Maimonides (1135–1204), who is famous for the *Guide for the Perplexed*, a book that tries to show that the ancient Torah is compatible with modern philosophy. Maimonides also drew up the 13 principles of the faith, which are a cornerstone of Jewish belief even today.

Spain also produced the mystical tradition known as the Kabbalah, which tries to go beyond mere intellect in search of a personal, spiritual union with God. The main Kabbalist text is the *Zohar* (Book of Divine Splendor), finished by Rabbi Moses de Leon of Granada (1250–1305). It sees God as *Eyn Sof*, or The Infinite One, and attributes to God specific characteristics (the ten *Sefirot* or "emanations"): the supreme crown of the divine name; wisdom; intelligence; love; power; beauty; endurance; majesty; foundation, and kingdom.

Below Jews are herded from the Warsaw Ghetto in 1943 by German SS soldiers. It is estimated that six million Jews were murdered in the Holocaust.

Dispersal again

The Christian conquest of Muslim Spain ended in 1492 when the Jews were forced to convert to Christianity or leave the country. Another dispersal followed, taking the Jews all around the Mediterranean and beyond. For the best part of two centuries, Jewish communities attempted to reconstruct and maintain themselves, but kept alive the hope that the Messiah would free them from their enemies and create a better world.

DIVISIONS IN JUDAISM

Throughout their long and often troubled history the Jews have tried to keep their identity as a people intact. However, being part of a family, they have sometimes had bitter family quarrels that have caused divisions among them. The principle theological divisions in our day are between Orthodox and non-Orthodox Jews.

Orthodox Judaism

Orthodox Judaism sees itself as the most authentic form of Jewish belief and practice, maintaining a tradition stretching back to Moses. Orthodox Jews cannot keep to all the 613 commandments because many relate to the era of the Temple, which has ceased to exist, but those they do keep have to be followed, however inconvenient this may be in the modern world.

At the end of the 1800s, a modern Orthodoxy emerged, encouraging Jews to break out of the ghetto (the section of a city to which Jews were restricted) and take part in the intellectual, political, and artistic life of the wider community while still remaining true to the Torah. It was now possible for a Jew to mix with mainstream society at school, university, or work and still be true to his or her Biblical inheritance.

One branch of Orthodoxy, known as Hasidism began in Poland and Germany in the 1700s. Even today, its members continue to follow the traditions and styles of dress of that era. They tend to live in close-knit communities centering on the home and synagogue. Their contact with modern Orthodox and non-Orthodox Jews may be limited. The best-known group is that of the Lubavitch, which thrives in New York.

Below Ethiopian Jews, or Falashas, airlifted to Israel in 1985, were thought by some to not be authentically Jewish. Many underwent "re-conversion" ceremonies to reaffirm their faith.

Reform Judaism

Also known as Progressive or Liberal Judaism, the Reform movement began in Germany early in the 1800s and spread in particular to the United States, where it is the dominant form of Judaism today. Followers do not believe that the Torah was "handed over" complete to Moses, but that it was written by humans with God's inspiration. For them, the attempt to work out God's will is an ongoing process.

Conservative Judaism

In the late 1800s, a new response to the challenges of modernity arose in the United States in the form of Conservative Judaism—which lies somewhere in between Orthodox and Progressive Judaism. The Conservative movement, and the Reconstructionist school that developed from it in the mid-1900s, observe most traditional laws and practices, and stress the community aspect of the faith.

Above The ultra-traditionalist community of Mea Sharim in Jerusalem keeps itself apart from mainstream society and retains its own distinct identity.

Zionism

Jerusalem was also known as the City of Zion, the name lent to the modern Zionist movement founded by an Austrian Jew, Theodor Herzl, in the late 1800s. He believed at first that Jews could flourish in any country, but changed his mind when he saw how deeply rooted anti-Semitism was. He therefore suggested establishing an independent homeland in Palestine. Some opposition came from Reform Jews, who felt that absorption into the wider society was healthier for Jewish culture, and also from some religious conservatives, who felt that no return to the land of Israel was possible until the Messiah had come. In 1948, the State of Israel came into being, but while its legitimacy is constantly being questioned by its Arab neighbors, it has offered Jews around the world a haven from persecution.

Right Modern Zionism championed the idea of an independent homeland for the Jews. These children carry the Israeli flag.

SACRED AND SECULAR

After the destruction of the Second Temple in A.D. 70 the Jews were scattered throughout the world. It would be almost 2,000 years before they would return to the Holy Land—to once again face the challenges of building an authentic Jewish homeland as a people "chosen by God."

The State of Israel

The State of Israel came into being by international decree on May 14, 1948, and was bitterly opposed by all the Arab nations. Many Palestinian Arabs were removed from their land and had their property seized to make way for incoming Jews, many of whom were survivors from the Nazi concentration camps and had no other homes to go to.

Could Arabs and Jews live side by side with equal rights and opportunities? Or should each group have a separate state to pursue a separate culture and a different religion? These are questions that still face the people of the Holy Land today. But if the differences between Jews and Arabs are clear, less clear (but just as great) are the differences between Jews and Jews.

Above These young Israelis are harvesting apples on a kibbutz, or collective farm. The kibbutz movement aims to create just and equal societies in microcosm. Kibbutzim were and are largely secular in nature and aim to distribute property and income according to the needs of the members.

Whose country?

Although they are an ancient people, Jews were given the opportunity in 1948 to build a brand-new society. But should it be a religious society ruled by the laws of God as they had been interpreted in the time of King Solomon? Or should it be a secular society giving people the freedom to practice the faith in the way that they wish (or even to reject it completely)?

The Orthodox Jewish authorities believe that they practice the only true form of Judaism and try to influence every aspect of civil life. This ranges from administering the rules surrounding marriage and divorce, to insisting that all commercial activity stops on the Sabbath, and crucially, in deciding who is or is not a true Jew.

Right Two Orthodox Jews stand alongside an Israeli soldier saying his prayers at Jerusalem's Wailing Wall.

Above Israel's parliament, the Knesset, is composed of secular and religious representatives who frequently argue over how much influence religion should have on everyday life.

As more and more Jews have come back to Israel from countries that have practiced different religious traditions or from former Communist countries that suppressed religion altogether, questions have been asked as to how Jewish the incomers really are.

NonOrthodox Jews resent the fact that the Orthodox authorities believe that they are the only ones who can decide, and growing tensions exist between the two groups.

Sacred or secular?

Not every Jew wants to live in a society governed by Biblical law, and many secular Jews are unhappy with the power that the religious parties have in the Israeli parliament, the Knesset. They accuse the religious groups of holding the country to ransom by offering to support this or that party in exchange for certain privileges—exemption from military service for religious students, for example, or money and resources for their religious schools.

But under the "Law of Return" all sides agree that every Jew from every corner of the world should have the right, if he or she wishes, to return to the historic and holy land of Israel.

GLOSSARY

Aggadah The narrative stories found in the Talmud.

Almighty God, the all-powerful.

Anoint To apply oil to a person as part of a ceremony to appoint a priest or a king.

Ark of the Covenant The golden box containing the Ten Commandments, originally kept in the Holy of Holies.

Ashkenazi A Jew of eastern or central European descent.

Avodah Jewish worship or service.

Bar Mitzvah A boy's spiritual passage into adulthood.

Bat Mitzvah A girl's spiritual passage into adulthood.

Chanukah The Jewish festival of lights.

Covenant A contract between two people, especially God and humanity.

Diaspora The Jewish community dispersed outside Israel.

Exile Expulsion from one's native land.

Exodus The flight of the Israelites from Egypt under the leadership of Moses.

Gemara Part of the Talmud containing a commentary on the Mishnah.

Gentile A nonJew.

Ghetto An area inhabited by one single community.

Hasidic Belonging to a vibrant and traditional branch of Judaism founded in the 1700s.

Halakah Jewish religious law.

High Priest The supreme head of the ancient Jewish priesthood.

Holocaust The Nazi extermination of more than six million Jews during the Second World War.

Holy of Holies The most sacred part of the Temple housing the Ark of the Covenant. Only the High Priest could enter.

Huppah A wedding canopy.

Idol A wooden or stone image of a god.

Immortality Everlasting life.

Kabbalah The ancient Jewish mystical tradition.

Kaddish The prayer of mourning.

Kibbutz A communal settlement.

Menorah A branched candlestick.

Messiah The savior of the Jewish people as foretold in the Hebrew Bible.

Midrash A way of interpreting Hebrew texts.

Minyan The minimum number of men required (ten) for worship to proceed.

Mishnah A collection of oral teachings and sayings.

Mitzvah A rule or religious requirement (plural; mitzvot).

Monotheism Belief in one god.

Mystical Concerned with intense spiritual experience.

Orthodox Judaism Traditional Judaism with a strict interpretation of Jewish law.

Passover The festival commemorating the deliverance of the Israelites, with God's help, from slavery in Egypt.

Patriarch A very important fatherlike figure, especially the founders of Judaism—Abraham, Isaac, and Jacob.

Pesach The Hebrew word for Passover.

Pharaoh An ancient Egyptian king.

Polytheism Worship of many gods.

Promised Land The land promised by God to Abraham and his descendants.

Prophet A person declaring God's purpose on Earth.

Psalms The sacred songs of the Hebrew Bible.

Reform Judaism A branch of Judaism interpreting Jewish law to fit in with modern society.

Revelation The disclosure of God's purpose in the world.

Rite A religious ritual.

Rosh Hashanah The Jewish New Year.

Sabbath In Jewish practice Saturday, the day of rest.

Sacrifice An offering to God.

Scroll A roll of paper containing a religious text.

Seder The Passover meal.

Sephardi A Jew of Mediterranean descent.

Shema The confession of faith that God is one.

Shiva The seven-day period of mourning after a funeral.

Shofar A ram's horn.

Sin An action deliberately contrary to the will of God.

Sukkot The festival of Tabernacles, five days after Yom Kippur, commemorating the Israelites' 40 years of wandering in the desert after they were led out of Egypt by Moses.

Synagogue A Jewish meeting place and place of worship.

Talmud The written text interpreting the Hebrew scriptures.

Tefillin Small boxes containing scriptural texts that Orthodox Jews strap to the arms and head during prayer.

Temple A building designed for worship, especially that built by King Solomon in Jerusalem.

Torah The first five books of the Hebrew Bible.

Unleavened Without yeast.

Wailing Wall Also the Western Wall, the visible remaining section of Solomon's Temple.

Yad A pointer used to prevent scrolls from being touched by fingers or hands.

Yeshiva A religious academy where the scriptures are studied.

Yom Kippur The Day of Atonement, when Jews fast and repent their sins.

Zionism The political movement to establish a Jewish homeland.

INDEX

ACKNOWLEDGMENTS

The publisher would like to thank the following for permission to reproduce their material. Every care has been taken to trace copyright holders. However, if there have been unintentional omissions or failure to trace copyright holders, we apologize and will, if informed, endeavor to make corrections in any future edition.

Cover main and inset Corbis; 1 Corbis; 6bl Format/Raissa Page; 6–7 Network/Gideon Mendel; 8bl Robert Harding/E. Simanor; 8–9 Michael Freeman; 9tr Sonia Halliday; 9bl Bridgeman Art Library; 10tr Bridgeman Art Library; 11tl Corbis; 11tr Corbis; 12r Art Archive; 13l Bridgeman Art Library; 18cl Format/Brenda Prince; 18br Rex Features; 18–19 Magnum Photos/Fred Mayer; 19bc E.T. Archive; 14tr Bridgeman Art Library/Musee Conde, Chantilly; 14bl E.T. Archive; 15 Bridgeman Art Library/Lambeth Palace Library, London; 16bl Sonia Halliday; 16–17 Roger Hutchins; 17tr Sygma/Jamel Balhi; 20tr Trip/H.Rogers; 20br Magnum Photos/Fred Mayer; 21tl Trip/E. James; 21b Hutchison Library/Liba Taylor; 22bl Format/Brenda Prince; 22-23 Sygma/J.P. Laffont; 23b Sygma/Daniel Mordzinski; 24bl Hutchison Library/Liba Taylor; 24-25 Trip/H.Rogers; 25br Hutchison Library/Liba Taylor; 26tr E.T. Archive/Bibliotheque de l'Arsenal, Paris; 26bc Trip/H. Rogers; 27bl Sonia Halliday/Barry Searle; 27tr Sygma/Daniel Mordzinski; 28–29 Corbis; 28bl Corbis; 29tr Corbis; 29bl Art Archive; 30tr Bridgeman Art Library/British Library; 30bl E.T. Archive; 31bl Keystone/Sygma; 32br Format/Meryl Levin; 32–33 Network/Barry Lewis; 33br Robert Harding/ASAP/Aliza Auerbach; 34tr Corbis; 34br Magnum Photos; 35t Reuters